YOUR KNOWLEDGE HAS VALUE

- We will publish your bachelor's and
  master's thesis, essays and papers

- Your own eBook and book -
  sold worldwide in all relevant shops

- Earn money with each sale

Upload your text at www.GRIN.com
and publish for free

Lora Cvetanova

King Kong in the city of New York. Kong's transformation from a "beast-god" on Scull Island to an attraction for the New York citizens

Plan for an oral presentation

GRIN Verlag

Bibliografische Information der Deutschen Nationalbibliothek:

Die Deutsche Bibliothek verzeichnet diese Publikation in der Deutschen National-
bibliografie; detaillierte bibliografische Daten sind im Internet über http://dnb.d-
nb.de/ abrufbar.

Imprint:

Copyright © 2014 GRIN Verlag GmbH
Druck und Bindung: Books on Demand GmbH, Norderstedt Germany
ISBN: 978-3-656-71986-1

This book at GRIN:

http://www.grin.com/en/e-book/278623/king-kong-in-the-city-of-new-york-kong-
s-transformation-from-a-beast-god

GRIN - Your knowledge has value

Der GRIN Verlag publiziert seit 1998 wissenschaftliche Arbeiten von Studenten, Hochschullehrern und anderen Akademikern als eBook und gedrucktes Buch. Die Verlagswebsite www.grin.com ist die ideale Plattform zur Veröffentlichung von Hausarbeiten, Abschlussarbeiten, wissenschaftlichen Aufsätzen, Dissertationen und Fachbüchern.

Visit us on the internet:

http://www.grin.com/

http://www.facebook.com/grincom

http://www.twitter.com/grin_com

Lora Cvetanova

Detailed plan with explanations for an oral presentation

University of Mirail

Toulouse /France

King Kong in the city of New York

Kong's transformation from a 'beast-god' on Scull Island,

to an attraction for the New York's citizens.

Comparative study of the original film King Kong and its novelization

May 2014

Contents

Detailed Plan for an Oral Presentation

Introduction:

The fallowing presentation will deal with King Kong's novelization of the movie script by Delos W. Lovelace (1932) and the 1933 classic film directed by Merian C. Cooper and Schoedsack.

1. General information about the film (came out during the great depression)
2. General information about the writing of the novelization (released one year before the film to advertise it)
3. Where did the idea of a movie with a giant gorilla come from (Cooper's fascination for adventures)

Willis O'Brien is the man primarily credited with bringing King Kong to the screen, but in truth, Kong was the brainchild of Merian Cooper, a truly larger-than-life film producer, on whom the character of Carl Denham was modeled. Cooper had been a fighter pilot in World War I, a POW after he was shot down behind enemy lines, and- with his partner Ernest Schoedsack- had traveled to the wilds of Asia and Africa to film documentaries.[1] Cooper imagined King Kong as the logical extension of his true life exploits; exaggerated but a recognizable caricature of his experiences. Originally he had wanted a "real gorilla to portray Kong, and even wanted to have it fight a Komodo dragon!"[2] We can all be grateful he encountered Willis O'Brien (who was working on his own dinosaur film-Creation) and decided to produce Kong and the monsters of Skull Island using stop-motion. The idea was "Cooper's, but the majesty and spectacle of the film belong to O'Brien. The miniature jungle settings created by O'Brien's crew with multiple glass paintings created an otherworldly quality to Skull Island that could not be duplicated by shooting on location- as Cooper had originally envisioned."[3]

To be sure, the film is very much a product of a simpler time. However, if the acting in Kong is compared to its early 1930's contemporaries in the horror/fantasy genre, it holds up quite well. Cooper and Schoedsack understood the necessity of establishing the characters before Kong's entrance, but kept dialog to a minimum. The story is told visually, with camera-work furthering plot points that may have seemed didactic otherwise. The film is carried by not only its visual imagery, but by one of the first feature length music scores. This was an innovation that put King Kong ahead its sound contemporaries, which relied quite heavily on the spoken word and direction alone. There is a ten minute sequence in the center of the film- after the death of the tyrannosaurus until

[1] http://www.imdb.com/title/tt0024216/reviews consulted on 15/06/2014 , at 15.03
[2] http://www.imdb.com/title/tt0024216/reviews consulted on 15/06/2014 , at 15.03

[3] http://www.imdb.com/title/tt0024216/reviews consulted on 15/06/2014 , at 15.03

the escape of Ann and Jack Driscoll (Bruce Cabot) from Kong's lair- that is told entirely with visuals, music, and sound effects. It is in large part due to the score that much of Kong's emotional impact is conveyed, particularly in its finale atop the Empire State Building. Steiner was able to suggest Kong's emotional state, assisting O'Brien in providing empathy to a creature who in reality was only an 18 inch high puppet.[4]

Like Star Wars, King Kong was a made for the movies myth, not based directly on any previous source other than Cooper and O'Brien's imagination. It spawned one of the first monster movie sequels, one remake, (so far) and countless imitations, parodies, and merchandise. Among fantasy films, only the Wizard of Oz can rival King Kong for the sheer longevity of popularity, but while Oz provided escapist entertainment, it did so in a lighter fashion. Kong provided escapism but of a more disturbing and haunting kind.

Part One: King Kong as 'a beast-god' on Scull Island.

He is powerful, immense and god like creature on his home island, there is no one bigger and stronger than him. He gains all battles and enjoys his victories.

Quote 1

'The beast–god lumbered back, beating his breast and indifferent to all his enemy's blows. His roaring charge carried both fighters hard against the tree in which Ann crouched and that long-tormented pedestal crashed dawn....Any critical observer would have realized that Kong had met enemies of the meat-eater breed before and had worked out a technique of battle which served well when he was not too enraged to use it.'[5](King Kong, chapter 13, p.100)

'When the meat-eater finally stretched out in death, Kong drew close and gazed down with loud cheeps of pleasure. He waggled the broken jaws with satisfaction and looked over towards Ann as though to invite her praise' (humanization of Kong - He needs Ann's approval and admiration) (King Kong, chapter 13, p.101)

'Driscoll had never thought to hear that thunder of rage without terror. But when it beat upon his ears, with its accompanying tattoo of mighty hand upon mighty chest, he was no more than a breach away from a supporting shout.' (King Kong, chapter 13, p. 116)

---

[4] http://www.torrentdownloads.me/torrent/494393/King+Kong+%281933%29+DVDRip+%28SiRiUs+sHaRe%29 consulted 14/06/2014, at 14.02

[5] Wallace, Edgar and Marian C. Cooper. *King Kong*, New York: The modern Library, 2005, p.13

6

7

---

[6] Image taken from http://sinemasaldunya.com/m-cooper-and-e-schoedsack-king-kong/ consulted
12/06/2014, 13.07
[7] Image taken from http://sinemasaldunya.com/m-cooper-and-e-schoedsack-king-kong/

Words used to describe Kong through the novelization of the movie script: Mighty hands, mighty chest, the beast-god, ape-beast, long flashing teeth, the beast's-god pillar-like legs, the great hands, huge fingers, the eighth wonder of the world, black monstrous body, etc.

Part Two: Kong as 'The Eighth Wonder of the world' in New York

Thanks to a long shot we see Kong at a stage in the center of the shot. Below we see the three human figures, which are small and insignificant, together with the part of the public. This makes a contrast of the big figure of Kong and suggest danger.

It is a mistake to compare Kong technically or artistically with films from later decades. Consider the cultural context in which King Kong was produced. America was in the darkest days of the Depression. World War II was seven years away, and nobody outside of a few physicists knew what 'atomic bomb' meant. Kong truly was the 'Eighth Wonder of the World' just as the Empire State Building was at the time considered the greatest technological marvel. As Cooper envisioned it, Kong was an adventure escapist film, offering Depression-Era audiences something that at the time would be considered the 'ultimate in adventure.' To today's audiences Kong no longer represents something 'all powerful' or able to 'lick the

---

[8] Image taken from http://sinemasaldunya.com/m-cooper-and-e-schoedsack-king-kong/ consulted 18/06/2014, 12.50

world' as Carl Denham described him back in 1933.In Kong's novelization Lovelace describes Kong's Presentation to the public as it fallows:

Quote 2
'*The crowd jammed four full blocks above Times Square and spilled over into the middles of Broadway. Traffic cops shook hopeless heads, twiddled helpless fingers and wearily motioned taxicabs into the side streets above and below. Where the crowed pressed thickest, filling not half but all the street, a sign hung high, announcing to the world in fiery letters: KING KONG, THE EIGHTH WONDER.*

Beneath the sign silk hats from Park Avenue jostled derbies from Bronx, Paris, gowns rustled against $3.98 pick-me-ups, sweaters rubbed dinner coats, slanted caps from Tenth Avenue scraped tip brims from Reverside Drive. The Social Register was there, and as representatives a delegation from the underworld as ever collected anywhere except at Police Headquarters on a morning after a clean –up. Intense young women from Greenwich Village were there, ant their earnest younger sisters from Columbia Heights. There were newsboys, peddlers, travelling salesmen, clerks, cashgirls, stenographers, debutantes, matrons, secretaries and Lilith-eyed maidens with no visible means of support. The whole town was there, waiting for the laggard attention of the ticket-taker and meanwhile staring up at: KING KONG, THE EIGHTH WONDER.' (King Kong, chapter eighteen, p. 138)

Yes, Kong has to lose his kingdom and his dignity to become entertainment for the riches in a big town so that he can find Ann and be with her. Kong is subdued and taken to the city, and we are introduced to a new character in the film: **NEW YORK CITY**. Here's one of the several posters of the era, showcasing Kong, Ann and the city of New York.

This is how we've learned how to see New York throughout the decades. As mean place, where people go to have their dreams come true. In this case is true to all of our main character. New York is where Ann is trying to make as an actress where Denham will succeed on his evil plot and where Kong goes to find Ann! And Eventually is destroyed by civilization and dies.

What is more, an element that adds dramatic grit to this action/fantasy horror movie is that it reflected the Great Depression. Denham needs a crew for an expedition to Africa's mysterious Skull Island. He needs a brave girl to be in his documentary footage. Ann Darrow (the most famous role **Fay Wray** would have in her long career), is so broke, hungry and down-on-her luck in Manhattan that she's caught stealing something to eat).In a way, that Depression era hit movie is practically an allegory for the black man in America. The script hints at our U.S. history of slavery and racism.

Carl Denham: "...there's something on that island that no white man has ever seen."[10]

Later, Kong is captured, cuffed and put on a boat. He'll be transported against his will from Africa to America where he will be used by a white guy for financial gain. When Denham declares "He's always been king of his world but we'll teach him fear," that is deep. You could've had that same exact line refer to a trapped African chieftain in *Roots* about to be forced onto a slave ship.[11]

Also, one of the most iconic scenes in film history is set here. 'The scene where Kong is at the top of the Empire State Building.

Part Three: Kong's destruction at Empire State Building. (novel) +Sequence analysis : The end of the movie . Kong at the Empire State Building. (Film)

At first, subdued and seemingly "civilized" by his captors, Kong breaks out into a deadly *Othello*-like rage when he sees Ann onstage with the man who took her away from him on the island. That man is now her fiance. Kong breaks out of his chains and all hell breaks lose in New York City. He's like a race riot unto himself. He finds and reclaims the thing he loves and heads for the now-famous finale on top of the Empire State Building.

a) Civilization against King Kong:

> *'The streets below New York were mobilizing for a fantastic, grim pursuit. From a score of waiting post police radio cars raced toward the hotel, their sirens screaming for clear traffic lanes.' (King Kong, chapter 19, p. 149)*

b) Kong climbs Empire State Building:

In July 1932, Schoedsack and his crew filmed establishing shots in the harbor of New York City. Fighter planes taking off and in flight were filmed at a U.S. Naval airfield in Brooklyn. Views of New York City were filmed from the Empire State Building
for backgrounds in the final scenes and architectural plans for the mooring mast were secured from the building's owners for a mock-up to be constructed on the Hollywood soundstage.

---

[10] Wallace, Edgar and Marian C. Cooper. King Kong, New York: The modern Library, 2005, 25

[11] http://bobbyriverstv.blogspot.fr/2012/11/race-and-king-kong-1933.html consulted 12/06/2014, 12.20

From a long shot and a low angle we see Empire State Building. Due to it the figure of Kong seems small and insignificant. Shot like that he seems harmless and an easy target for the palanes which are about to shoot at him .The Empite State Building is in the centre of the shot, showing its magnificence and importance for New York.

Here Kong is almost at the top. We see the planes coming. We can't see the rest of the city because of the clouds which creates a sense of mystery and danger.

[12] Image taken from
http://fr.images.search.yahoo.com/yhs/search;_ylt=A0LEVry0uuBTgBsAf.GPAwx.;_ylu=X3oDMTBsa3ZzMnBvBH NIYwNzYwRjb2xvA2JmMQR2dGlkAw--?_adv_prop=image&fr=yhs-ironsource-fullyhosted_003&va=king+kong&hspart=ironsource&hsimp=yhs-fullyhosted_003

13

In the novelization, the following dialog remind us of the scene where Kong climbs Empire State Building. Driscoll and Denham refer to Kong with the words 'his figure seemed smaller than that of a man', 'a black silhouette', 'he crawed'. It is natural for him to look for a shelter at the highest place as he often did on Scull iskalnd, Remember! His cave is at the top of the mountain. 'and still he crawled'- usually we use crawle for insects, here the author uses crawled to show once again Kong's insignificants and to remind the reader that the end will be unhappy.

Quote

'You will never catch King Kong on any roof' he cried furiously.

'He is going to the top of the mountain, I tell you'

Kong was so high now that his figure seemed smaller than that of a man, and still he climbed. A black silhouette against the chalky walls he drew himself from ledge to ledge until he rose into the bright flood flights which swept around the crest of the building and still he crawled.'(King Kong, chapter 19, p. 153)

c) Kong fights the planes:

Contrary to the first shots I've discussed, here the composition is central. Thanks to a standard close shot, the spectator feels closer to Kong. Even though he is high , this time he is not the king of the island , and the planes are stonger then him. The battle is uneven. Kong is one against six. He is all alone at the top of the building, with his enemies surrounding him, guns firing all the time, and the city bellow, waiting for his downfall.

[14] Iamge taken from
http://fr.images.search.yahoo.com/yhs/search;_ylt=A0LEVryOuuBTgBsAf.GPAwx.;_ylu=X3oDMTBsa3ZzMnBvBH NlYwNzYwRjb2xvA2JmMQR2dGlkAw--?_adv_prop=image&fr=yhs-ironsource-fullyhosted_003&va=king+kong&hspart=ironsource&hsimp=yhs-fullyhosted_003

[15] Iamge taken from
http://fr.images.search.yahoo.com/yhs/search;_ylt=A0LEVry0uuBTgBsAf.GPAwx.;_ylu=X3oDMTBsa3ZzMnBvBH NlYwNzYwRjb2xvA2JmMQR2dGlkAw--?_adv_prop=image&fr=yhs-ironsource-fullyhosted_003&va=king+kong&hspart=ironsource&hsimp=yhs-fullyhosted_003

Quote

'The second plane had cut in close, obviously meaning to brush Kong with a wing tip. As the plane curved, its wing missed. It was Kong who struck the blow. His great paw swung out and struck....'(King Kong, chapter 19, p. 154)

'The plane came down in a long swift slide. For a split second it seemed to poise, like a giant humming bird, in the front of its beast adversary; then it curved upward and was away.' (King Kong, chapter 19, p. 155)

    d) King Kong loses the battle with civilization and dies:

        Whether in the jungle threatened by extinct pre-historic creatures or at the very top of the Empire State Building, Ann Darrow will survive and be protected by King Kong until he dies. Denham the promoter, at the body of his fatally wounded captive and star, delivers one of my favorite lines in a famous Hollywood film: "It was beauty killed the beast."

Spectators at the time, just after the WW1 and in the middle of the great depression probably needed to re reassure that the American nation will survive any kind of danger. A War, an economic depression, an invasion and so all, will be crushed and Americans will prevail. The unhappy ending for Kong shows the fear of the people at the time of the unknown and of the different. Kong is destined to die, so that civilization can triumph and americans can be reassured that there is no danger, that there are people (like Dahnam and Driscall) who will fight for them and protect them.

'The rattle of the successive machine guns grew louder over Kong's tattooing... He fought to the end. With his last strength he leaped from the rearmost plane as it curved away. He missed but, his mighty spring carried him clear of the setbacks below, and out above the street. For a breath then, high above civilization which had destroyed him, he hung in same regal loneliness that had been his upon Scull Mountain Island. Then he plunged down in wreckage at the feet of his conquerors.'(King Kong, chapter 19, p. 156)

Conclusion

1. Movement from the Island into the city
2. The main character Kong undergoes changes(from a mighty beast to a creature kept in captivity)
3. Once liberated in a new environment Kong cannot adapt, he looks for the biggest thing to climb, just as he would do as if he were on the island looking for protection, and a place to hide.
4. The civilization and the city destroy him
5. Humans are the bad one while Kong is humanized loving Ann, civilasion for Kong means Death or captivity. The smart, creative direction made the giant beast horrifying yet human.
6. Humans (plains) mean danger and death.
7. Shows that it is not easy to survive in the big city.

Simplified plan

Introduction:

I. Part One: King Kong as 'a beast-god' on Scull Island. He is powerful, immense and god like creature on his home island, there is no one bigger and stronger than him. He gains all battles and enjoys his victories.

Quote 1

'The beast–god lumbered back, beating his breast and indifferent to all his enemy's blows. His roaring charge carried both fighters hard against the tree in which Ann crouched and that long-tormented pedestal crashed dawn....Any critical observer would have realized that Kong had met enemies of the meat-eater breed before and had worked out a technique of battle which served well when he was not too enraged to use it.'(King Kong, chapter 13, p.100)

'When the meat-eater finally stretched out in death, Kong drew close and gazed down with loud cheeps of pleasure. He waggled the broken jaws with satisfaction and looked over towards Ann as though to invite her praise' (humanization of Kong - He needs Ann's approval and admiration) (King Kong, chapter 13, p.101)

'Driscoll had never thought to hear that thunder of rage without terror. But when it beat upon his ears, with its accompanying tattoo of mighty hand upon mighty chest, he was no more than a breach away from a supporting shout.' (King Kong, chapter 13, p. 116)

Words used to describe Kong through the novelization of the movie script: Mighty hands, mighty chest, the beast-god, ape-beast, long flashing teeth, the beast's-god pillar-like legs, the great hands, huge fingers, the eighth wonder of the world, black monstrous body, etc.

II. Part Two: Kong as ' The Eighth Wonder of the world' in New York
Quote 2

'The crowd jammed four full blocks above Times Square and spilled over into the middles of Broadway. Traffic cops shook hopeless heads, twiddled helpless fingers and wearily motioned taxicabs into the side streets above and below. Where the crowed pressed thickest, filling not half but all the street, a sign hung high, announcing to the world in fiery letters: KONG KONG, THE EIGHTH WONDER.

Beneath the sign silk hats from Park Avenue jostled derbies from Bronx, Paris, gowns rustled against $3.98 pick-me-ups, sweaters rubbed dinner coats, slanted caps from Tenth Avenue scraped tip brims from Reverside Drive. The Social Register was there, and as representatives a delegation from the underworld as ever collected anywhere except at Police Headquarters on a morning after a clean –up. Intense young women from Greenwich Village were there, ant their earnest younger sisters from Columbia Heights. There were newsboys, peddlers, travelling salesmen, clerks, cashgirls, stenographers, debutantes, matrons, secretaries and Lilith-eyed maidens with no visible means of support. The whole town was there, waiting for the laggard attention of the ticket-taker and meanwhile staring up at: KING KONG, THE EIGHTH WONDER.' (King Kong, chapter eighteen, p.138)

III. Part Three: Kong's destruction at Empire State Building. (novel) +Sequence analysis : The end of the movie . Kong at the Empire state building.(Film)

a) Civilization against King Kong:
Quote 3

'The streets below New York were mobilizing for a fantastic, grim pursuit. From a score of waiting post police radio cars raced toward the hotel, their sirens screaming for clear traffic lanes.' (King Kong, chapter 19, p. 149)

b) *Kong climbs Empire State Building:*

Quote 4

> *'You will never catch King Kong on any roof' he cried furiously.*

> *'He is going to the top of the mountain, I tell you'*

> *Kong was so high now that his figure seemed smaller than that of a man, and still he climbed. A black silhouette against the chalky walls he drew himself from ledge to ledge until he rose into the bright flood flights which swept around the crest of the building and still he crawled.' (King Kong, chapter 19, p. 153)*

c)   Kong fights the planes:
Quote 5

'The second plane had cut in close, obviously meaning to brush Kong with a wing tip. As the plane curved, its wing missed. It was Kong who struck the blow. His great paw swung out and struck....' (King Kong, chapter 19, p. 154)

'The plane came down in a long swift slide. For a split second it seemed to poise, like a giant humming bird, in the front of its beast adversary; then it curved upward and was away.' (King Kong, chapter 19, p. 155)

d)   King Kong loses the battle with civilization and dies:
Quote 6

'The rattle of the successive machine guns grew louder over Kong's tattooing... He fought to the end. With his last strength he leaped from the rearmost plane as it curved away. He missed but, his mighty spring carried him clear of the setbacks below, and out above the street. For a breath then, high above civilization which had destroyed him, he hung in same regal loneliness that had been his upon Scull Mountain Island. Then he plunged down in wreckage at the feet of his conquerors.' (King Kong, chapter 19, p. 156)

Conclusion

Bibliography

Primary Sources

Book

Wallace, Edgar and Marian C. Cooper. *King Kong, New York: The modern Library, 2005*

Novelization: Lovelace, Delos M.

Film

Cooper, Merian C. and Earnest B. Schoedsack. *King Kong. Aries/RKO (1933)*

All images are taken from google images and are used only for educational means and should be considered only as appropriate for this study.

Secondary Sources

 Beaver, Frank. *Dictionary of Film Terms-The Aesthetic Companion to film Analysis. New York: Twayne Publishers, 1994*

Clarke, David B. ed. *The cinematic City. Londres et New York: Routledge, 1997*

Dick, B.F. *Anatomy of Film. Bedford/St. Martin's, 1995*

Kracauer, Siegfried. *Theory of Film. New York: Oxford University Press, 1960*

Mennel, Barbara. *Cities and the Cinema. Londres et New York: Routledge, 2008*

Monaco, James. *How to Read a Film: Movies, Media, Multimedia. Oxford: Oxford University Press, 2000*

Shiel,Mark et Tony Fitzmaurice. *Cinema and the City: Film and the City. Londres et New York: Routledge, 200*